INNOVATORS

Stephenie Meyer

Twilight Saga Author

Other titles in the Innovators series include:

Stephenie Meyer

Twilight Saga Author

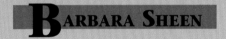

BARBARA SHEEN

KIDHAVEN PRESS

A part of Gale, Cengage Learning

GALE
CENGAGE Learning™

Detroit • New York • San Francisco • New Haven, Conn • Waterville, Maine • London

GALE
CENGAGE Learning™

LIBRARY OF CONGRESS CATALOGING-IN-PUBLICATION DATA

Sheen, Barbara.
  Stephenie Meyer : Twilight saga author / by Barbara Sheen.
      p. cm. -- (Innovators)
  Includes bibliographical references and index.
  ISBN 978-0-7377-5066-9 (hardcover)
  1. Meyer, Stephenie, 1973---Juvenile literature. 2. Authors, American--21st century--Biography--Juvenile literature. 3. Young adult fiction--Authorship--Juvenile literature. I. Title.
  PS3613.E979Z885 2010
  813'.6--dc22
  [B]
                                                                            2009048397

KidHaven Press
27500 Drake Rd.
Farmington Hills, MI 48331

ISBN-13: 978-0-7377-5066-9
ISBN-10: 0-7377-5066-9

Printed in the United States of America
2 3 4 5 6 7 14 13 12 11

Printed by Bang Printing, Brainerd, MN, 2nd Ptg., 07/2011

CONTENTS

INTRODUCTION

Not Your Usual Vampire Tale

Frightening stories and the monsters that populate them have always captured people's imagination. Those that concern vampires are among the most popular. From ancient legends about creatures that feed on the blood of the living, to the villains of horror movies, the idea of vampires fascinates us. Oddly enough, author Stephenie Meyer, whose *Twilight Saga* features vampires, never shared this fascination. She does not like violent or frightening stories. "I'm not a vampire fan," she says. "I haven't read Dracula, and I don't watch scary movies."[1]

She prefers stories that feature **fantasy** and romance to horror, and suspense to **graphic violence**. In the *Twilight Saga*, she created a new kind of vampire that reflects her taste. Although the Cullen clan, the saga's vampire family, is extremely powerful, they do not drink human blood or sleep in coffins. They do not have fangs, fly like bats, or burn to death in sunlight. Instead, they sparkle. "I don't think my books are going to be really graphic or dark, because of who I am. There's always going to be a lot of light in my stories,"[2] she explains.

The Joy of Reading

In truth, the *Twilight Saga* is more about growing up, falling in love, and making choices than it is about monsters. By combining these themes with her special vampires and the magical world they inhabit, Meyer created a series of four books called the *Twilight Saga*, which readers throughout the world find irresistible.

Stephenie Meyer was always an avid reader, but had never written anything herself before *Twilight*.

More than 70 millions copies of the *Twilight Saga* have been sold. The series has a huge following, especially among tween and teenage girls. Many of these young people were not enthusiastic readers before they started reading the series. Reading was something they did for school, not for entertainment or pleasure. The *Twilight Saga* changed that. It made reading fun. Young people did not mind reading these long books. They wanted to. Then they wanted to talk about what they read with each other, and with Meyer. They wanted to write their own stories featuring the series' characters, too.

As an **avid** reader herself, Meyer is thrilled that she has helped spread the joy of reading: "I don't know what to say when a parent comes up to me and says 'My daughter was not reading and now she is.' Books were my whole life. That was my favorite thing in the whole world. The fact that I can open that door up for somebody—if even for one person—is amazing."[3]

CHAPTER 1

An Ordinary Life

Stephenie Morgan was born on Christmas Eve, December 24, 1973, in Hartford, Connecticut, to Candy and Stephen Morgan. Stephenie was named after her father, which explains the unusual spelling of her name. She was the second of six children, having three brothers and two sisters. When she was four years old, the family moved to a house on the outskirts of Phoenix, Arizona. It was here that she grew up.

Stephenie led a fairly ordinary life. Many of the things that shaped her life also influenced her writing.

A Close-Knit Group

The Morgans were a close-knit family whose **Mormon** religion played an important role in their lives. They spent three hours in church every Sunday and tried to incorporate their religious beliefs into everything they did. Today, many of these values run through Stephenie's writing. For example, the idea of making

Meyer was raised in the outskirts of Phoenix, Arizona.

decisions and having free will is an important part of her religion and a theme in all her work.

In addition to church activities, the family spent a lot of time having fun together. The older children, like Stephenie, took care of the younger ones. "I think that coming from such a large family has given me a lot of insight into different personality types," she says. "My **siblings** sometimes crop up as characters in my stories."[4]

Sneaking Away

One of the family's favorite activities happened before bedtime, when the children gathered in the hall between the bedrooms and their father read to them. Stephenie, a self-described bookworm, loved this time. She adored reading and being read to. Her dad did not select typical children's books to read aloud.

Instead he chose **science fiction** or fantasy books that he wanted to read.

Stephenie's dad knew how to capture his audience's imagination. He would always stop reading at the most exciting part, leaving Stephenie eager to know what was going to happen. The next day she would snatch the book from her father's study, hide in a closet, and read ahead. "I always had this sense that reading was an exciting thing, and I loved big, fat books,"[5] she says.

Stephenie's mother preferred classic romances like *Gone with the Wind*, *Romeo and Juliet*, and *Pride and Prejudice* to fantasies and science fiction. She had a large collection of books, which Stephenie read over and over. At the time, Stephenie did not realize

As a young girl, Meyer would sneak into the closet in her father's study to read stories.

what a big impact her parents' taste in **literature** would have on her. But in the future, she would combine fantasy and romance in her *Twilight Saga*.

Making Up Stories

When Stephenie was not reading, she was busy making up stories. She did this to entertain herself, especially on the frequent road trips the family took to visit relatives in Salt Lake City, Utah. She never told her stories to anyone or wrote them down. Stephenie did not have a lot of self-confidence. She was afraid that if she told her stories to her brothers and sisters they would laugh at her. "My whole life I told myself stories," she explains. "I just didn't think that anyone would want to hear them. I was very insecure."[6]

A Regular Girl

Her active imagination and love of reading helped make Stephenie a good student. Academically, she got good grades and won a college scholarship. Socially, like Bella, the heroine of the *Twilight Saga*, she was insecure and a little clumsy. In fact, she modeled some of Bella's life experiences after her own. For instance, just as Bella did not become popular until she moved to Forks (a small logging town in Washington State where the books take place), Meyer was not popular until she went away to college. And, like Bella, Meyer was confused by her newfound social status. She explains:

> Some parts of Bella's experience are modeled after real life (my life, to be exact) . . . I modeled Bella's move to Forks after my real life move from high school to college . . . In high school I was a mousy A-track

wallflower . . . Then I went to college in Provo, Utah. Let me tell you my stock went through the roof. See, beauty is a lot more subjective than you think . . . I had dates every weekend with lots of really pretty and intelligent boys (some of whose names end up in my books). It was quite confusing at first, because I knew there was nothing different about me.[7]

Just as Bella's years in Forks High School were happy ones, so too were Stephenie's years in college. After graduating from high school in 1991, Stephenie went to Brigham Young University where she majored in English, concentrating on literature rather than creative writing. It was a perfect course of study for a bookworm. "I don't know if I ever considered anything else,"

Meyer majored in English at Brigham Young University in Salt Lake City, Utah.

she explains. "That's what I love. I love reading, and this was a major I could read in."[8]

She did a little writing in college but rarely finished what she started. Nor, did she share her work with others because she was afraid they would not like it.

Getting Married

In the summer before her senior year, Stephenie started dating

Meyer and husband "Pancho" were married in 1994 when she was twenty-one years old. Here they are at the premier of the *Twilight* movie.

Christian "Pancho" Meyer. The two met in church when they were children but they never socialized before. One day they started talking and realized that they liked each other. In fact, Pancho liked Stephenie so much that he proposed to her on their second date and kept proposing on every date thereafter. "It's funny because in 20 years of knowing each other, we never had a conversation. But we got along so well. On our second official date was when he proposed. He proposed a lot. Over 40 times. He would propose every night and I would tell him no every night. It was kind of our end-of-date thing,"[9] she explains.

Nine months later, Stephenie finally said yes. The two were married in 1994. Once Stephenie graduated from college in 1995, they settled in a Phoenix suburb very close to both their families. At 21 years old, Stephenie was ready to begin a new stage in her life. She had no idea how exciting it was going to be.

CHAPTER 2

It Started with a Dream

After she graduated from college, Stephenie worked as a receptionist in a real estate office. Once her son Gabe was born, she became a full-time mom. Within the next four years, she had two more sons, Seth and Eli.

Stephenie led a busy life similar to that of many young mothers. Then, one night she had an extraordinary dream. It changed her life in ways she could not even imagine.

"You Only Get One Dream Like That in a Lifetime"

It was June 2, 2003. Meyer remembers the date because it was the day her sons, then ages one, two, and five, started swimming lessons. That night she had a vivid dream. According to Meyer:

> In my dream two people were having this intense conversation in a meadow in the woods. One of these people was just your average girl. The other person was fantastically beautiful, sparkly, and a vampire.

The idea for *Twilight* came in a dream to Meyer, where a young girl and vampire fall in love. Adapted to film, the characters are portrayed by Robert Pattinson and Kristen Stewart.

They were discussing the difficulties inherent in the facts that A) they were falling in love with each other while B) the vampire was particularly attracted to the scent of her blood, and was having difficulties restraining himself from killing her immediately.[10]

When Stephenie woke up, she could not get the dream out of her head. "I think you only get one dream like that in a lifetime,"[11] she says.

She lay in bed thinking about it. It was so interesting that she did not want to forget it, so she decided to write it down. She recalls what happened:

> Though I had a million things to do . . . I stayed in bed thinking about the dream. I was so intrigued by the nameless couple's story that I hated the idea of forgetting it . . . I eventually got up and did the immediate necessities, and then . . . sat down at the computer to write . . . I didn't want to lose the dream, so I typed out as much as I could remember.[12]

That day between swimming lessons, housekeeping, and caring for her sons, Meyer managed to type ten pages. They would become chapter 13 of *Twilight*.

All Consuming

Those pages were just the start. The young couple, whom she named Edward and Bella, fascinated Stephenie. She wanted to know what happened to them. Since there was no book to steal away with to find out, she had to make it up. In much the same way that she made up stories as a child, she made up this story. But this time she wrote it down.

Meyer could not get away from *Twilight*. Even when she was not writing she was thinking about it, especially its setting in the Olympic Rainforest of Washington.

For the next three months, she spent every spare minute writing. With three small children to take care of, this was not easy. She set up a desk in the middle of the family room so she could watch her sons while she worked, but they constantly interrupted her. Mainly, she worked at night. She got very little sleep.

> I did a lot of the writing at night, because after they were in bed was the best time to concentrate. But during the day, I really couldn't stay away from the computer, so I was up and down a lot. I'd sit down and write a few lines, and then I'd get up and give somebody juice, then sit down and write a few more

lines, and then go change a diaper . . . On a good day I would write 10 or 12 pages, single-spaced.[13]

When she was not writing she was thinking about it. Bella and Edward had become almost as real to her as her own family. She loved them and could not stop thinking about them or the world they lived in. She thought about the plot while her children were swimming. Then, she rushed home and typed. She kept a notepad on her nightstand to jot down ideas that popped into her head when she finally got to bed. "Bella and Edward were, quite literally, voices in my head," she explains. "They simply wouldn't shut up . . . It was your typical Arizona summer, hot, sunny, . . . but when I think back to those three months I remember rain and cool green things, like I really spent the summer in the Olympic Rainforest [*Twilight's* setting]."[14]

A Secret Revealed

Meyer was so busy writing that she lost touch with her friends and her siblings. She did not tell anyone what she was doing. "I was really protective and shy about it because it's a vampire romance. It's still embarrassing to say those words—It sounds so cheesy,"[15] she says.

When Stephenie stopped calling, her older sister, Emily, became concerned. The two were extremely close. Stephenie had never kept a secret from her before. When Emily pressed her, Stephenie revealed her secret. Emily was intrigued. Soon Stephenie was e-mailing her page after page. Emily loved it and kept asking for more.

Sending It Out

It took Stephenie three months to finish *Twilight*. She never thought about getting it published. She wrote the book to entertain herself. It was Emily who put the idea of trying to get

Of the fifteen letters Meyer sent, Jodi Reamer at Writer's House in New York City is the only agent who offered to represent her.

the book published into Meyer's head. Meyer reluctantly agreed. She explains: "It certainly wasn't belief in my fabulous talent that pushed me forward. I think it was just that I loved my characters so much, and so they were real to me and I wanted other people to know them too."[16]

Stephenie knew nothing about the publishing process. She used the Internet to find out what to do. She soon had a list of publishers and **literary agents**. She sent out fifteen **query letters**. Just dropping them in the mailbox made Stephenie nervous. "I didn't plan to start a new career when I did this, and it took a lot of courage to send out those query letters. I sent fifteen, and I got nine rejection letters, five no response, and one person who wanted to see me,"[17] she explains.

That person was Jodi Reamer, a well-known and successful literary agent at Writers House. In October 2003, she offered to represent Meyer. Stephenie could hardly believe it. She would have been even more surprised if she had known what was to come.

CHAPTER 3

Twilight Mania

With Reamer's help, Stephenie spent the next few weeks getting Twilight ready to send to publishers. At the same time, Meyer was busily working on an **epilogue** to *Twilight*. Instead of an epilogue this became *New Moon*, the second title in the *Twilight* series. She would go on to write a total of four books in the series: *Twilight*, *New Moon*, *Eclipse*, and *Breaking Dawn*. They would come to be known as the *Twilight Saga*. Reamer was confident she could sell *Twilight*, but neither she nor Meyer had any idea what a phenomenon it would become.

A Book Deal

Reamer sent *Twilight* to nine publishing houses. Right before Thanksgiving 2003, Little Brown and Company said they wanted to publish it. Stephenie was hoping to be paid a few thousand dollars for the book. That would be enough money to help pay off the loan on the Meyer's minivan. She was stunned when Little

Within weeks of its release in October of 2005, *Twilight* was number five on the New York Times bestseller list. By fall 2009, more than 17 million copies of the book had been sold.

Brown offered her $300,000 for a three book deal. She was even more shocked when Reamer turned Little Brown down, asking for one million dollars instead. According to Meyer, when Reamer turned down all that money, "I almost threw up."[18]

Reamer knew what she was doing. Little Brown wound up paying Meyer $750,000 for the first three books in the *Twilight Saga*. That was the largest sum of money the company ever paid a first-time author.

It was six months since Meyer wrote her first words. Those words were not only going to be published, Stephenie was being paid an enormous sum of money for them. She could not believe it. "It felt very strange, like some sort of practical joke for a while,"[19] she explains.

Twilighters

Twilight was in bookstores on October 5, 2005. Within weeks of its release, it was number five on the *New York Times* bestseller list, and it received critical praise from many book reviewers. By fall 2009, more than 17 million copies of the book had been sold. Many readers became passionate about it. They were enchanted with the world Meyer had created and the characters who populated it. Calling themselves Twilighters, they posted on social networks like MySpace where they connected with each other, holding online discussions about every aspect of the book. Many of these pages became so popular that their creators set up Web sites to host them. One, which eventually became the Twilight Moms (twilightmoms.com) Web site, drew over 60,000 friends on MySpace.

Meyer was thrilled that so many people loved her characters as much as she did, and she reached out to her fans. For in-

Fans have flocked to Forks, Washington, where *Twilight* takes place. Here, a group of fans on a tour visit the house portrayed as the Cullen residence.

stance, although Meyer had never visited MySpace before, when she heard about a *Twilight* discussion group there, she became a friend and participated in the site, interacting with her fans in a very personal way. She answered their questions, commented on **fan fiction**, and welcomed feedback on her own work. In fact, she even set up her own MySpace page.

She also set up her own Web site, StephenieMeyer.com. Here, she not only issued news about book tours, readings, and events she was participating in, she also welcomed her fans into her life. She posted chatty letters about herself and pictures of her family. She even put up her e-mail address. Although she received thousands of e-mails, she tried to answer each and every one personally.

All this interaction spurred book sales. It also formed a unique bond between the Twilighters, and between Meyer and her fans. They shared a magical world. Through this world they all became virtual friends.

Like a Rock Star

Meyer also connected with her fans through guest appearances on television shows, and by doing readings in bookstores and libraries throughout the United States. As time went on, more and more people turned out for her appearances. It was not uncommon for long lines to snake around bookstores in anticipation of her appearances. Her appearances became so popular that they had to be limited to places that could hold thousands of fans. And, when she appeared to greet her fans, they became hysterical,

Meyer is amazed and flattered by the attention she gets from fans wherever she goes.

screaming and carrying on like audiences at a rock concert. Meyer was amazed and flattered by their devotion: "It's kind of cool. No one's ever accused the Twilighters of not being passionate, and it makes me feel really good that they care so much about everything,"[20] she says.

At one reading a fan suggested Meyer organize a prom for fans similar to the one depicted in *Twilight*. With the help of her publisher, Meyer began organizing the event. When the prom was announced on her Web site, it sold out within six hours. The demand was so great that she organized a second prom, which also sold out. Each prom was limited to five hundred people. The events were held at Arizona State University in May 2007. Guests dressed as their favorite *Twilight* characters. Two actors portraying *Twilight* characters Edward and Jacob were present, as was Meyer dressed as Bella. She selected all the music for the events, chatted with fans, and signed so many copies of *Eclipse*, which had just come out, that she got a blister on her finger.

The idea of a prom so excited Twilighters that satellite proms were held throughout the world at the same time.

New Moon, Eclipse, and *Breaking Dawn*

During all this time, Stephenie never stopped writing. In 2006, *New Moon* was released. *Eclipse* and *Breaking Dawn* followed in 2007 and 2009. In all, the series spent a combined 143 weeks on the *New York Times* bestseller list. In addition, the books claimed the top four slots in *USA Today's* 2008 year-end bestseller list. Meyer was the first author ever to achieve this.

The fourth installment in the *Twilight Saga* is *Breaking Dawn*, which published in 2009.

The books have been translated into 38 languages and have won many awards including the 2009 Kid's Choice Award. As of September 2009, more than 70 million copies of the *Twilight Saga* have been sold.

In a few short years, Meyer went from being a young mother who told herself stories to a celebrated author and multimillionaire. She still cannot believe what happened. "When *Twilight* hit the *New York Times* bestseller list at number 5, for me that was the pinnacle, that was the moment," she says. "I never thought I would be there. And I keep having moments like that . . . it just keeps being huge . . . I had no idea. I still have no idea."[21]

CHAPTER 4

Branching Out

The incredible success of the *Twilight Saga* opened many doors for Meyer, allowing her to take on new projects in a variety of media.

Bringing the *Twilight Saga* to the Big Screen

One project involved turning the *Twilight Saga* into a series of movies. *Twilight* the movie opened in theaters November 2008. *New Moon* followed in November 2009, with movie versions of the other books scheduled for the future. Experts in the movie industry predicted the first movie, *Twilight*, would draw a largely female audience and would not make much money. They were soon proven wrong.

Although the movie was made on a low budget, it debuted as number one in box office sales. It made more than 70 million dollars in its first weekend and over 340 million dollars in its

When you can live forever,
what do you live for?

Twilight was brought to the big screen in 2008. Meyer made a cameo appearance, and was very pleased with the film overall.

twilight

IN THEATRES
11·21·08

first three months. It received good reviews and won the 2009 MTV Movie Award for best movie.

Meyer did not write the script, but she did have a lot of input on it. She also talked with the actors about the characters and made a **cameo appearance** in the movie. Still, she worried about how the movie would turn out. When she saw it for the first time, she realized her fears were groundless. This is what happened: "I was so worried that it was going to be horrible and break my heart," she recalls. "They put it on and . . . I was so involved. The characters were speaking the way they should and the heart was there. I could have watched it all night."[22]

Midnight Sun

Another project involved retelling *Twilight* from Edward's point of view in a book called *Midnight Sun*. Meyer had written twelve chapters of the book when her work was released onto the Internet by an unknown source. After *Twilight* was published and Meyer became more confident about her writing, she often shared her work-in-progress with her friends. This act of betrayal hurt her. "I never felt any anger, actually. Just a lot of sadness," she says. "I mean it was a sucker punch—like someone came up behind you and just hammered you in the kidneys and you had no idea it was coming."[23]

As a result, Meyer put the book aside. She is unsure if she will ever finish it. She also became more secretive about her work and her personal life, both because of what happened with *Midnight Sun* and because her huge popularity was becoming hard to cope with. She removed her MySpace page and her personal e-mail address from her Web site. She even stopped reading the chapters she was working on aloud to her sons at

Meyer wrote twelve chapters to a book that was to be titled *Midnight Sun* and told from Edward's point of view, but it was leaked to the Internet and Meyer shelved the project.

night, a practice she started after *Twilight's* publication. She worried that they might accidentally reveal the plot to their friends.

New Directions

With *Midnight Sun* out of the picture, Meyer turned her attention to another book she had been working on, *The Host*. There were no vampires in this story. It was geared towards adults rather than young people. But, like the *Twilight Saga*, it was unusual in that it combined science fiction and romance. *The Host* is about an alien parasite that takes over a woman's body and then falls in love with the woman's boyfriend. Meyer came up with the idea for the book while driving from Phoenix to Salt Lake City, in much the same way she came up with stories on family road trips as a little girl. She explains: "I was on this horrible boring drive from Phoenix to Salt Lake City . . . I was completely on my own and bored out of my mind. I tend to tell myself stories in those situations, and I just caught myself in the middle of an idea about two people sharing a body, both in love with the same guy."[24]

The Host was released in May 2008. Even though Meyer felt that it was her best writing to date, she worried that her fans would not like it. In an interview on Amazon.com before the book's release she explained: "I really hope my existing fans of the *Twilight Saga* will enjoy *The Host*. . . . I'm a little worried. There's a

Meyer's novel *The Host* published in May 2008, and was geared toward a more adult audience with themes of science fiction and romance.

chance they're going to open the book up, start flipping through and say there's no Edward here and then they'll toss it off the balcony."[25]

Meyer had nothing to worry about. The book debuted as number one on the *New York Times* bestseller list and stayed on the list for twenty-six weeks. Not only did Meyer's existing fans like it, but it brought her new fans. In addition, Meyer has become involved in designing a line of shirts and skateboard decks, featuring images of aliens based on the book, for Hobo Skate Company. Profits from this merchandise will go to charities that help the homeless.

This is not the only charity Meyer has been involved with. In 2009, she helped organize "Save the Book Babe," an event that raised money for breast cancer.

Into the Future

Meyer has lots of other projects, too. She is involved in turning *The Host* into a movie. She also is writing *Stephenie's Sanctum, Monster Manual III* for the fourth edition of the Dungeon and Dragons video game. In this manual, Meyer has created new and different monsters to accompany the popular game. One is Uniman, a half-man, half-unicorn that shoots rainbows from its eyes. Meyer is very excited about this project: "The most joyful time writing the *Twilight* series was when I transformed the vampire and werewolf . . . into something exciting and new," she explains. "I can't wait to do the same with dragons, trolls, and purple worms."[26]

In addition, Meyer is writing and directing "The Resolution," a music video from American rock band Jack's Mannequin. Meyer listens to music as she writes, and she posts a

In addition to writing, Meyer has taken on other interests, such as directing a music video for the band Jack's Mannequin.

playlist for each of her books on her Web site. The list contains the names of songs that inspired her as she wrote. Working on a music video seems a logical next step.

Of course, she is also writing. She is considering writing a **sequel** to *The Host*, and she is working on a story about ghosts. Then, there is a story about mermaids, and a third about time travel. "Now that I've found out that people actually like my stories," she says, "it's definitely not a problem coming up with ideas about what to write next."[27]

One thing is certain, whatever Meyer chooses to write, her work is likely to intrigue and enchant readers for many years to come.

NOTES

Introduction: Not Your Usual Vampire Tale

1. Quoted in Jeffrey A. Trachtenberg, "Booksellers Find Life After Harry in Vampire Novel," *Wall Street Journal,* August 10, 2007, p. B1.

2. Quoted in Tony-Allen Mills, "News Review Interview: Stephenie Meyer," *Times Online*, August 10, 2008. http://entertainment.timesonline.co.uk/tol/arts_and_entertainment/books/article4492238.ece.

3. Quoted in Joel D. Amos, "Stephenie Meyer Speaks," She-Knows.com. http://www.sheknows.com/articles/804082.htm?page=2.

Chapter 1: An Ordinary Life

4. Quoted in Cynthia Leitich Smith, "Author Interview: Stephenie Meyer on Twilight," Cynsations, March 27, 2006. http://cynthialeitichsmith.blogspot.com/2006/03/author-interview-stephenie-meyer-on.html.

5. Quoted in Mills, "News Review Interview: Stephenie Meyer."

6. Quoted in Mills, "News Review Interview: Stephenie Meyer."

7. Quoted in "Frequently Asked Questions, Twilight," StephenieMeyer.com. www.stepheniemeyer.com/twilight_faq.html#tips.

8. Quoted in Megan Irwin, "Charmed: Stephenie Meyer's Vampire Romance Novels Made a Mormon Mom an International Sensation," *Phoenix New Times,* July 12, 2008. http://www.phoenixnewtimes.com/2007-07-12/news/charmed.

9. Quoted in Irwin, "Charmed."

Chapter 2: It Started with a Dream

10. Quoted in "Dreamcatcher," *Vogue*, March 2009, p. 448.

11. Quoted in "10 Questions for Stephenie Meyer," *Time*, September 1, 2008, p. 4.

12. Quoted in "The Story Behind Twilight," StephenieMeyer.com. www.StephenieMeyer.com/twilight.html.

13. Quoted in Rick Margolis, "Love at First Bite," *School Library Journal*, October 2005, p. 37.

14. Quoted in "The Story Behind Twilight."

15. Quoted in Irwin, "Charmed."

16. Quoted in "The Story Behind Twilight."

17. Quoted in "10 Questions for Stephenie Meyer."

Chapter 3: Twilight Mania

18. Quoted in Irwin, "Charmed."

19. Quoted in Irwin, "Charmed."

20. Quoted in Heather Green, "Harry Potter with Fangs—And a Social Network," *Business Week*, August 11, 2008, p. 44.

21. Quoted in "10 Questions for Stephenie Meyer."

Chapter 4: Branching Out

22. Quoted in Karen Valby, "Stephenie Meyer Talks Twilight," EW.com, November 5, 2008. www.ew.com/ew/

article/0,,20234559_20234567_20238527,00.html.

23. Quoted in Valby, "Stephenie Meyer Talks Twilight."

24. Quoted in Larry Carroll, "'Twilight' Writer Stephenie Meyer Wants Matt Damon for 'Host' Movie, Discusses Her Rabid Fanbase," MTV.com, April 9. 2008. www.mtv.com/movies/news/articles/1585112/story.jhtml.

25. Quoted in "Amazon Exclusive: Stephenie Meyer Talks About The Host," Amazon.com. www.amazon.com/Host-Novel-Stephenie-Meyer/dp/0316068047/ref=ntt_at_ep_dpi_6.

26. Quoted in Brian Briggs, "Wizards of the Coast Taps Stephenie Meyer to Write Monster Manual III," Bbspot, August 12, 2009. www.bbspot.com/News/2009/08/stephenie-meyer-monster-manual.html.

27. Quoted in Mills, "News Review Interview: Stephenie Meyer."

GLOSSARY

avid: Enthusiastic or eager.

cameo appearance: A brief appearance by a famous person in a movie.

epilogue: A brief section at the end of a book that tells the fate of the characters.

fan fiction: Stories written by fans featuring characters from books, movies, or television.

fantasy: Fiction that features magic or the supernatural.

graphic violence: Vivid, realistic acts of violence in books, movies, or television.

literary agents: People who represent authors to publishers.

literature: Highly valued written work.

Mormon: A religious group.

query letters: Letters to publishers or literary agents describing a manuscript.

science fiction: Fiction that features scientific elements.

sequel: A story that continues the story started in an earlier work.

siblings: Brothers and sisters.

For Further Exploration

Books

Ryan Burton and Adam Gragg, *Female Force Bestsellers: Stephenie Meyer*. Bellingham, WA: Bluewater Production, 2009. Short biography of Meyer in comic book form.

Stephenie Meyer, *Twilight*. New York: Little Brown, 2005. The first book in the *Twilight Saga*.

Raymond H. Miller, *Vampires*. Farmington Hills, MI: Kidhaven Books, 2004. Information about the vampire myth including its origin.

Article

"10 Questions for Stephenie Meyer," *Time*, September 1, 2008.

Web Sites

The Official Web site of Stephenie Meyer (http://www.StephenieMeyer.com/index.html). This is Meyer's official Web site. It has information about her life, books, movies, and upcoming events. Meyer posts notes to her fans here.

Twilight Lexicon (http://www.twilightlexicon.com/). A Twilighters Web site with tons of information about vampires, werewolves, the *Twilight Saga*, the movies, and links.

Twilighters.org (http://twilighters.org/). A fan site with lots of pictures and information about the books, movies, Meyer, and Forks, Washington.

INDEX

PICTURE CREDITS

ABOUT THE AUTHOR

Barbara Sheen is the author of more than 50 books for young people. She lives in New Mexico with her family. In her spare time, she likes to swim, cook, garden, and walk. Of course, she loves to read and really enjoyed the *Twilight Saga*.